D0477715

Win
a Nut

Written by Roderick Hunt
Illustrated by Nick Schon,
based on the original characters
created by Roderick Hunt and Alex Brychta

OXFORD
UNIVERSITY PRESS

Read these words

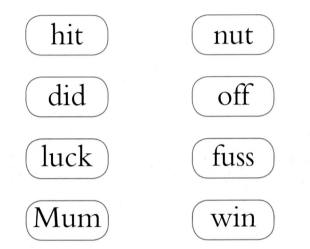

hit

did

luck

Mum

nut

off

fuss

win

Can Dad hit a nut?

Dad hit a nut.

It did not fall off.

Can Mum win a nut?

Mum hit a nut, but it did not
fall off.

Chip had a go.

Chip hit a nut!

The nut fell off.

Talk about the story

Who tried to win a coconut first?

Did Mum hit a coconut?

Why did Chip ask 'Is it a fix?'

What games have you played at a fair?

Missing letters

Choose the letters to make a word:

i u ff

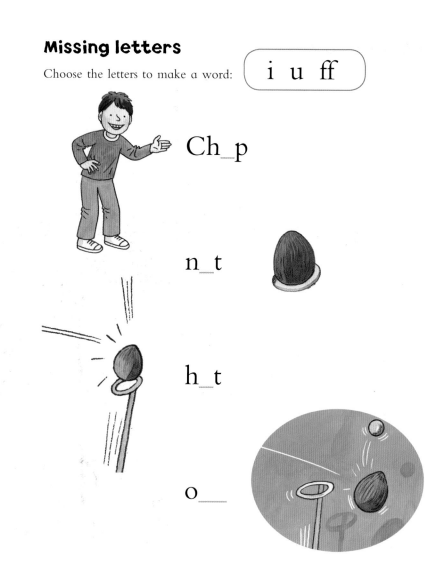

Ch_p

n_t

h_t

o___

Who did what?

Match each person to the thing they did.

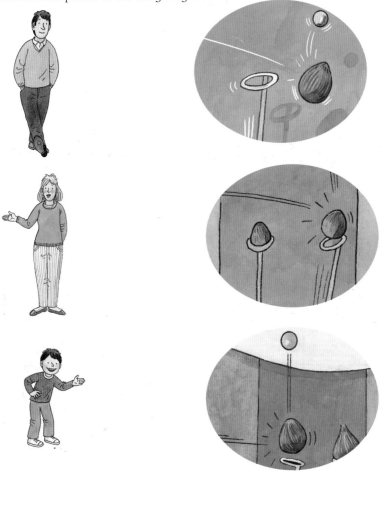

The Bag on the Bus

Written by Roderick Hunt
Illustrated by Nick Schon,
based on the original characters
created by Roderick Hunt and Alex Brychta

OXFORD
UNIVERSITY PRESS

Read these words

bus   run

stop   fun

hop   got

bag   ran

Mum and Biff got off the bus.

Mum's bag was on the bus.

My laptop is in the bag!

Mum ran and Biff ran.

Dad and Kipper ran.

Chip and Floppy ran.

Mum's bag is on the bus.

Mum got to the bus stop.

24

Mum got her bag back ...

Mum got her laptop back.

Talk about the story

Who got off the bus?

What was in Mum's bag?

Why did Mum say it was no fun?

What kinds of things have you lost?

Missing letters

Choose the letters to make a word:

u   s

bu_

r_n

_top

f_n

Word search

How many words can you find with *r*, *u*, *s* or *ff* in them?

Can you write them down?

b	u	s	u	s
p	r	a	n	v
o	f	f	t	n
a	p	u	f	f
b	r	u	n	t

Mum's maze

Help Mum get to her bag.